BRAND PLAN SELLING

The Co-op Coach's Sensible Solution to Unlocking the Mysteries of Co-op Advertising

by Tim Marceau, The Co-op Coach

For information about this title or to order other books and/or electronic media, contact the publisher:
Cooperative [media] Solutions
1287 River Road, Waterbury, VT 05676
802-777-9096
tim@cooperativemediasolutions.com

ISBN: 978-1-4699496-4-2

Printed in the United States of America

Cover design by: Elizabeth Tomsuden
Editing: Sue Publicover
Interior design by: 1106 Design

Table of Contents

Having traveled thousands of miles across the country and spending countless days meeting with retailers in both big cities and small, there is one thing I know to be true. In every region, in every community, there are retailers carrying brand name products and they have earned co-op funds that can be spent with your media, without fail, without exception, without a doubt.

se·ri·ous·ly?

To a large or great degree or extent
• I think you are *seriously* mistaken. • During her first year in the United States, she was *seriously* [=*very, extremely*] unhappy. • She's a *seriously* beautiful woman. [=a very beautiful woman]

"*Seriously, what part of your brain were you using when you thought that would work?*"

I was asked that very question before and had to give it some serious thought. We should all consider this question right now. What parts of your brain do you suppose you are using in your everyday selling?

Einstein said, "The definition of insanity is doing the same thing over and over and expecting different results." But it doesn't take a genius to know that if you continue to do what you have always done, you will continue to get what you have always got. Is that good enough for you? Are you will to accept what you have always got or do you want more?

In the current economy you can be assured your bosses are asking for more revenue every year. How are you going to deliver? Where on earth will you find this new source of revenue? Do you want to double your sales and income?

If you do, then you need
BRAND PLAN SELLING

We all recognize brands; we're exposed to thousands of them every day. From brushing your teeth to choosing your clothes to reading a magazine or the hordes of emails in your inbox, consumers are exposed to an endless tsunami of brand impressions.

> *Did you know that manufacturers make billions—yes, billions, with a "b"—of dollars available annually for your local and regional clients to use on advertising with your medium?*

Start tuning into those brands that you are surrounded with and the opportunities for marketing dollars for your prospects and advertisers abound. Often times they are literally right in front of you.

Did you know that manufacturers make billions—yes, billions, with a "b"—of dollars available annually for your local and regional clients to use on advertising with your medium? Over one-third of those funds go unused every year, so let's get you your fair share of this money.

In this guide, you'll learn a step-by-step process for:

- Recognizing brand funding co-opportunities
- Engaging your client or prospect in the co-op conversation
- Speaking the co-op language fluently
- Understanding co-op terms and plans
- Tapping into those funds easily for both you and your advertiser.

Are you ready to start closing using Brand Plan Selling? Then roll up your sleeves and let's get started.

con·nect

To have or establish a rapport
<tried to *connect* with the younger generation> :
to place or establish in relationship

irst and foremost, before we engage a prospect in a discussion regarding co-opportunities, we need to connect. We all have some common ground with every prospect and, let's face it, at the end of the day, people buy from people they like and trust.

After having had thousands of cold calls with sellers in markets nationwide, one thing has become abundantly clear to me: We all have universal commonalities. Find that commonality and bridge the gap with that conversation before you delve into facts and figures and ask your prospect for personal account information. Do they have children or grandchildren? Are they active? Do they volunteer? Are they a sports fanatic? I guarantee you that with a quick scan of their office you can find evidence of a commonality. I know we are all busy with deadlines looming and budgets to be met, but these few extra minutes spent bridging the gap with a new prospect will pay off.

be·gin·ning

The point or time at which
something begins : a starting point — usually
singular ▪ He has been working there since the
beginning of the year. ▪ A poem was recited at
the *beginning* of the wedding ceremony. ▪ It was
clear **from the (very) beginning** that she would
eventually succeed. ▪ The company was very
small **in the beginning** [=when it began], but it
eventually became a giant corporation.

I remember the moment the light bulb went off over
my head, that moment when it became infinitely
clear that I had been missing a huge selling opportunity. I was at a sales seminar for the newspaper
where I worked as a Retail Sales Representative. I was
attending a round table session about co-op advertising. Of course at the time, we didn't have the benefit
of computers and the Internet and the process was
cumbersome, but it was still a revelation. I simply
couldn't believe that manufacturers were offering all

of this money to my prospects and I was not aware of it—worse yet, my prospects were not aware of it, at least not aware enough to mention it when we were discussing marketing budgets. It turns out they were as afraid of the process as I was unaware.

Never lose sight of the fact that you are learning to prospect and sell with a new resource, but you are not in the business of selling co-op. You are in the business of selling your product. You will use your newfound knowledge of co-op advertising to help you close deals by overcoming budget objections or to double the proposed sale by using brands and brand funding in your advertising campaigns

I came back from that conference convinced that the concept of co-op advertising was going to take me to the next level in my sales career. I immediately started researching co-op advertising and how we could put a real initiative in place. As I became more co-op-aware, I began recognizing brands everywhere—the copier at work, my watch, the calculator, my office furniture, my shoes, and the prospects I had that sold apparel, automobiles, kitchen cabinets. It was like an awakening! I was surrounded by co-opportunity, but didn't have the knowledge or resources to tap into it—well, not yet.

The process of selling the idea to have an internal co-op department at the newspaper started with putting together a proposal to the Powers That Be. I clearly proved the return on investment would be realized within months of contracting with a database provider and training our sales staff. That was then. You, however, in this day and age, can start your own co-op initiative without having to sell the idea on your superiors and, better yet, at no cost.

How? You need to learn to the basic infrastructure of how to use co-op advertising, and how to engage your prospects in the conversation. I use simplified techniques with my clients as The Co-Op Coach, nationwide, every day, and we create millions of dollars in found co-op advertising revenue annually. Once you start the conversation with your advertising sales prospect, you will be amazed at how open they are to sharing details and contacting manufacturers with you.

Never lose sight of the fact that you are learning to prospect and sell with a new resource, but you are not in the business of selling co-op. You are in the business of selling your product. You will use your newfound knowledge of co-op advertising to help you close deals by overcoming budget objections or to double the proposed sale by using brands and brand funding in your advertising campaigns.

EDUCATE THE PROSPECT ON YOUR MEDIA TYPE

Often you have prospected from another media source and you might be talking with a client who uses one media as their primary source of advertising. With your first contact, you need to discuss the benefits of advertising with your media type. Always engage in a conversation a bout the advantages of having a healthy media mix in their marketing plans. Remind your prospect—without being condescending—that using multiple media platforms consistently reinforces their message across multiple channels and is essential to effective brand building.

DISCUSS YOUR MEDIA OR MARKETING PRODUCT

Now we can get down to the details, discussing what sets you apart from the others, such as your media or marketing opportunities. Prospects are not looking to be sold. In fact, they often set up barriers against it. They want you to respect their valuable time and give them something worthy in return. Become a knowledgeable marketing consultant, not an order-taker. Educate them on all the opportunities available in your region and thoroughly explain what makes you the best choice. Your product is the best, right? Be prepared to support that firm belief. Be proud and, most importantly, know your product and be confident, as Forrest Gump said, "If you can't sing good, sing loud!"

SELL YOURSELF

Why? Retailers are overwhelmed with trying to overcome the challenges of selling themselves to their customers. Then, minutes after they open the door to potential shoppers, they are met with the onslaught of salespeople who enter their store as an uninvited guest. They are not there to fill the retailer's cash register but are interrupting their attempt to do so—at least, this is how most reps are perceived.

You're not only distracting them from their desired tasks, but also asking them to change the way they are currently doing business. Imagine the frustration of being approached a half a dozen times a day with a steady drone of cloned sales pitches. I remember one retailer showing me a sign they had behind the register that said, "Every third salesman will be shot and bad news, number two just left!" E!" ducate them, become a valuable, trusted resource for advertising advice. With the high turnover in sales you may be the second or third salesperson they have seen in one year from the same company, you need to convince them that you are going to be around long after the first sale is closed. Do not baffle them with bull, dazzle them with your knowledge.

SELL USING CO-OP

Now and only now are you ready to introduce the concept of using co-op funding to offset your potential client's cost of advertising with you. You need to make sure your prospect is interested and showing the buying signs before you start to dig deeper, calling manufacturers with them to locate funds. You have nothing to lose by starting the co-op advertising discovery process if your prospect is simply stuck on a budget objection. If they object to your product or service, however, then you have more work to do before you introduce co-op into the discussion. You can't give sell them on a great deal if you haven't sold them on the product.

co·op·er·a·tive

Involving two or more people or groups working together to do something · a *cooperative* [=*joint, combined*] effort/venture

WHAT IS CO-OP ADVERTISING?

o-op advertising represents a partnership between the manufacturer and the retailer. They are sharing the cost of local advertising. Thousands of manufacturers have co-op plans that guarantee your prospects will be reimbursed up to a certain amount of funds for advertising expressly to promote that manufacturer's product. The co-op funds are a percentage of dollar value of goods purchased (e.g., two percent of the total product purchased in a quarter). Reimbursements generally vary from 50 to 100 percent with 50 percent reimbursement being the most common.

You must always be painfully aware that this arrangement is between the manufacturer and the retailer, not between you and the manufacturer. The manufacturer's customer is the retailer, the retailer is the one the manufacturer wants to have the con-

> *Co-op advertising represents a partnership between the manufacturer and the retailer. They are sharing the cost of local advertising. Thousands of manufacturers have co-op plans that guarantee your prospects will be reimbursed up to a certain amount of funds for advertising expressly to promote that manufacturer's product.*

versation with regarding available funding and availability of preapproved marketing materials. They're not interested in your stake. So, it is crucial that you get buy-in from the retailer on every step of the process. You must make the calls to the manufacturer with your retailer present. It's a collaborative effort and you can't remove anyone from the process if you want a win for everyone concerned.

SHIFT YOUR MINDSET

Tune yourself in to being more brand aware in your daily sales calls. What percentage of your local and regional advertisers do you suppose you have in your territory that sell brands and have co-op funds available? Are you targeting prospects where the owner or decision-maker is is on site? The best way to tap into available funding is to have "buy in" and full cooperation from the owner will assure you that they will be forthcoming with information regarding manufacturer contact information. You need this information to assist them in locating their funds.

It's time to get excited as you are about to jump-start your new sales initiative using co-op. You can realistically expect to create 20 percent more revenue year over year using these new techniques. Nationally statistics tell us that you will close slightly less than 2 out of every 10 calls. Through co-op awareness when you

Through co-op awareness when you are prospecting we can't increase your close ratio but what we can do is give you twice as many prospects, thereby doubling your sales.

are prospecting we can't increase your close ratio but what we can do is give you twice as many prospects, thereby doubling your sales.

It never ceases to amaze me to continually meet prospects who have not taken advantage of co-opportunities that are readily available to them. How can that be? The information simply isn't disseminated to them in a way that makes them comfortable with the process; thus, they waste all that available co-op funding. Your job is to change that. By understanding the language of co-op advertising, you will be completely comfortable explaining exactly what needs to be done to build co-op compliant advertising. You can also share details on what the client needs to do to ensure speedy and guaranteed reimbursement.

Just the other day on a cold call with a seller, we dropped in unannounced on a local flooring and carpeting retailer. The retailer was displaying a Mohawk Color Center neon sign in the front window. This sign was a sure signal that this prospect had potential funding. After introducing ourselves to the owner, the seller was able to talk about the features and benefits of advertising with their media. Once the prospect was engaged and showed interest, I introduced possible co-op funds to help offset the cost of advertising.

The prospect was very forthcoming with information—so much so, that she excused herself and brought back all of the co-op information she had received from the manufacturer, including co-op plan details and pre-approved ad copy. With one simple call to the manufacturer from the prospect, her funds were located and she was off and running with her new, local, targeted ad campaign. Sometimes it simply is a matter of introducing the subject! Once you cross that threshold, you would be amazed at how often the prospect will openly share the information they have on hand.

HOW MUCH MONEY IS THERE?

How much co-op funding is available in your sales territory? The formula is pretty straight-forward. For reasonable estimates, take the population of your territory and multiply it by $30 per person. *For example: you have 100,000 people that live in the area that your media reaches.*

$$100,000 \times \$30. = \$3,000,000$$

Knowing that more than one-third of co-op advertising goes unused annually that means more than $1 million dollars is left on the manufacturer's table. It is waiting for you to meet with your prospects and educate them on how to tap into these funds before they expire yet again.

> *How much co-op funding is available in your sales territory? The formula is pretty straight-forward. For reasonable estimates, take the population of your territory and multiply it by $30 per person.*

PAYMENT DUE

Your retailer will be responsible for the after-sale paperwork as well for submitting the reimbursement claim to the manufacturer. It will serve you well to be straight-forward with your client. Be clear that even though you are partnering with them on the process of tapping into available co-op funds, at the end of the day, it is their responsibility to follow through with the execution.

Once the retailer has run advertising with your media, they are responsible for paying your invoice in a timely manner. They then submit the claim to the manufacturer for reimbursement. You are not a bank and cannot hold an extended note on the debt to your company. If the client objects to paying your invoice before they receive reimbursement—which can take months, depending on the manufacturer—then they are not a quality prospect. If the prospect cannot float the funds for that time, they were likely not going to pay you anyway. It's may be hard to come to terms with the fact that even though a prospect has available manufacturer funding they may not be a quality, long term prospect, but you need to make this distinction, or pay the price, literally.

WHERE DO UNUSED CO-OP FUNDS GO?

What happens to those funds? NOTHING! Unused co-op funds simply expire. Manufacturers do not generally roll these funds over. It's up to you as a sales professional to speak with prospects about taking back their funds and advertising before their earned rewards disappear. Remind your prospect that the cost of co-op advertising is built in to the cost of the product. It is not a gift. The funds belong to them once they fulfill the buying criteria, but in order to claim co-op dollars, they need to advertise. Like a tax return, retailers are paying in to the co-op account all throughout the year, but if a retailer doesn't place a claim (tax return), there's no refund.

rec·og·nize

To acknowledge or take notice
of in some definite way: to perceive clearly:
REALIZE

How do you recognize brand opportunities? They are all around you. We are exposed to over 5,000 brand messages a day. Many are subliminal but a vast number of these messages are right in front of us. Just like with any media message, consumers "tune in" when they are in the buying cycle and tune out when they're not. Our job is to put that brand in front of them, convince them of the features and benefits, so that when the consumer is in the buying cycle, they will choose the brand that they have been most exposed to—the one that remains at the top of their minds.

The best way to approach brand awareness for prospecting purposes is to explore categories that generally have co-op funds attached. Think about the products that you personally are going to be in the market for over the next six months and make a list. Those are your best prospects. Will you need a new automobile, auto service, heating and air conditioning, lawn care, or home improvement products like hardware, decking, and paint? Likely yes and guess what? They all have co-op funding available for various media.

PROSPECTING TIP FOR BRAND PLAN SELLING

Below each category under Brand Plan Selling Leads I have given you three starter manufactures that offer formal co-op plans. On the manufacturer's homepage, find the link for "Find a Retailer", "Where to Buy", "Locate a Store Near You", or a similar search link. It is usually fairly easy to see this link because the manufacturers want to drive leads to their local retailers. You'll probably have to enter your zip code and a mileage search radius. Then simply print the list of retailers in your area and visit them to start the conversation regarding offsetting the cost of advertising with you by using available co-op funding.

Automobiles

What will compel an automotive buyer? Solid advertising campaigns featuring the brand will create traffic at the dealership. Use the manufacturer funding to help offset the cost of getting the message out about new body styles, special financing programs, rates, rebates, inventory, and all with the manufacturer reimbursing your prospects 50% to 100%, depending on the make, model, and the time of year.

Most new car manufacturers have formal, paying co-op programs. I would caution you to not approach an auto dealer about educating them on available funding. Most dealers have what is referred to as a "dealer dashboard" from the brand manufacturer. The dashboard includes their current co-op accrual, how much and when funds expire, pre-approved advertising materials, and more. Your process here should let them know that you; (1) are aware of the co-op; (2) will assure that only preapproved materials with appropriate, timely offers and disclaimers will run; and (3) will obtain the necessary paperwork for submitting the claim—an extra copy of your invoice, affidavit for proof of performance, a tearsheet for print media or script for radio or television—at the end of the month in which the advertising runs, assuring them speedy reimbursement. Offering this service will build your credibility of the co-op process and establish you as a valuable marketing partner, not an order-taker.

If a dealer is not willing to share the accrual amount, ask a salesperson how many new automobile units they sold last year. Take $200 per unit as an average accrual to give you an estimated co-op fund amount. Many automobile manufacturers reimburse at 50%, so the marketing budget would be twice that number. For example: Your dealer prospect sold 1,000 units last year, giving them an estimated $200,000 co-op accrual balance to spend with all media buys. If the manufacturer reimburses at 50%, your dealer has a budget of $400,000, with half of that being reimbursed after proof of approved advertising. If your dealer prospect is reimbursed at 100%, their annual co-op marketing budget is $200,000 with all of it being reimbursed after proof of approved advertising.

Automotive Brand Plan Selling Leads

Chevrolet   Ford   BMW

Automotive Service

As salespeople, we realize how valuable our automobiles are. Many of us have an office on wheels and realize that proper maintenance and upkeep is essential to our livelihood. Most consumers' cars are equally important to them; if they are made aware of the value of regular maintenance through effective, branded advertising, they are more likely to invest in preventative procedures.

Automotive Service is one of the most neglected brand-funded co-op categories of all. When we are prospecting and doggedly seeking out the New Car Sales Manager, how often do we forego calling on the Service and Parts Department Manger? Almost always! The average driver spends approximately $1,200 annually on automotive maintenance, thus funneling a tremendous amount of money towards branded automotive service products, which results in significant accruals for your prospects.

There is a separate pool of co-op funds available solely for parts and service advertising and promotions. They have an important message of their own to deliver about the value of automotive service. New car dealers' service departments will service any make and model. They will often run oil and lube change specials or parts specials in an effort to bring new customers in to the dealership. Once these customers cross this threshold, the dealership has an opportunity to showcase the dealership, meet the staff, and expose these prospects to the new car models. The goal is to open their minds to the idea of buying their next new or used automobile from this dealership.

The next time you pass the car dealership that you have been prospecting—perhaps unsuccessfully for years—pull over, go to the Parts and Service Department, and visit with the Service Manager. He or she has sales goals to reach, much like the Sales Department. They are always looking for a creative way to drive additional traffic and generate new revenue by being able to provide and up-sell both emergency service and scheduled maintenance.

Automotive Service Brand Plan Selling Leads
*GM Parts and Service   Toyota Parts and Service
Bridgestone Tire*

Kitchen and Bathroom Cabinetry

Co-op accrual is based on price and turn. The average kitchen remodel cost in the United States is in excess of $58,000. Most major cabinet manufacturers have formal co-op plans. You should prospect independent cabinet retailers who represent national cabinet brands. Many retailers manufacture their own custom cabinetry in which case they do not accrue funds. Some retailers offer cabinet refacing, which is not a brand prospect for co-op funding either. Accessories like knobs and drawer slides have formal programs, but you want to inquire with your client about their sales volume as 1% of knob sales from one manufacturer would not amount to a reasonable accrual to offset the cost of featuring that product in an advertising campaign.

At the same time, many of the kitchen and bathroom cabinetry retailers stock "go with" items that have significant brand funding, like major appliances, countertops, sinks and faucets, furniture, window coverings, and more. Don't miss the opportunity to talk to them about these additional co-op opportunities. You will be pleasantly surprised how many local, independent kitchen cabinet retailers you have in your areas that represent famous brand names.

Kitchen and Bathroom Cabinetry
Brand Plan Selling Leads
Bertch Vanities and Cabinets   Kraftmaid Cabinetry
Aristokraft Cabinets

Lawn and Garden

Homeowners spend an estimated 45 billion dollars annually on lawn and landscaping services and products. Lawn and Garden brands tend to be seasonal, so as an experienced seller, you know that you need to be prospecting six months prior to the season. Advertising decisions are being made in January and February for campaigns to run heavily in March, April, and May. There are very strong programs offered in the Spring and Summer for power equipment like push lawnmowers, riding lawnmowers, lawn fertilizers, paving blocks and co-op programs for Fall and Winter with snow blowers, salt, shovels, and portable and whole home power generator brands.

Lawn and Garden Brand Plan Selling Leads

*Scotts Lawn and Garden   Kubota Tractor
Generac Power Systems*

Power Sports

You know the brands. You pass the dealerships every day. Today is the day you start being more co-op aware, tuning into the signage around you, and making sure you stop to have the advertising conversation about using brands to offset the bottom line—and to bring them in. Most brands in the power sports category pay in excess of 50%, so don't undersell yourself! Make sure your initial "ask" is double the size or frequency that you would normally propose, assuming a generous manufacturer reimbursement.

The Power Sports category includes scooters, motorcycles, ATVs, and watercraft. Motorcycles have become an increasingly popular mode of transportation as the price of gasoline has steadily risen. According to the Department of Transportation, there are currently more than four million motorcycles registered in the United States today.

Prospects that carry power sports brands are key to building a relationship with a retailer/dealer who has product to advertise year round; i.e., your local motorcycle dealer also sells ATVs, personal watercraft, and snowmobiles—something for every season. Most of the manufacturers' brands have ongoing promotions for you to feature including low financing incentives, low down payments, long-term financing, and manufacturer rebates. The devils in the details with power sports advertising—pay particular attention to the disclaimers and never run with an ad that has not been pre-approved by the manufacture co-op administrator.

Power Sports Brand Plan Selling Leads
Arctic Cat   Harley Davidson   Polaris

Footwear and Apparel

Most footwear retailers place early pre-season orders, so funding is earned long before the season to advertise the footwear arrives. Every community has independent footwear and clothing retailers that carry top quality, nationally known, and trusted brands. Make visiting these retailers a priority as they are the kings of "turn"—constantly re-ordering to maintain minimum inventory level means footwear retailers are consistently earning new co-op funds!

Footwear and Apparel Brand Plan Selling Leads
*Columbia Sportswear   The North Face
Dansko Footwear*

Major Appliances

Think about your territory. How many local-owned, independently-operated electronics stores do you have? I would venture a guess that it's not many. Most of that business was overrun by the big box stores that offered these products at reduced prices (and small profit margins), making it virtually impossible for the local electronics store to stay in business. As electronics became more disposable and the constant demand for new technology ramped up, our television repair shops simply disappeared in many markets.

Not so with our major appliance dealers. They were prepared for the competition and rose to the challenge of the big box retailers coming into their areas. How did they do so well? By banding together and forming regional buying groups. These groups are owned and operated by the participating members and all of the co-op accruals that are earned are passed through to each retailer, based on their purchases from each manufacturer. They receive a monthly statement with the current earned accruals for each brand. This combined buying power, along with manufacturer rebates, has helped them keep pace in the pricing wars with larger, national major appliance retailers. To step up the strength of their groups—and offer the lowest pricing for independent stores—many of these regional buying groups have banded together under a national umbrella.

Major Appliance Brand Plan Selling Leads

General Electric   Whirlpool Appliances   KitchenAid

Heating and Air Conditioning

Americans spend over $3,000 dollars a year to heat and air condition their homes, so low maintenance and newer, more energy efficient units have gained value. Every region of the country has dozens of retailers and installers that are prime prospects to target for advertising with accrued co-op funds from the HVAC distributor. If I had to pick one category to work, it would be HVAC. Why? Manufacturer co-op funds are generously passed through distributor networks in most cases. Most communities have multiple, independent installers. Accrued funds are significant. Many HVAC manufacturers now have marketing web portals that only require your installer prospect to sign up for a username and password to access the site's preapproved advertising materials.

> • *What brand do you sell the most?*
>
> • *What is the name of your distributor?*
>
> • *May I have the contact information of your distributor sales representatives?*

We often find that the owner is actively working in the field—making it difficult to connect—but you can facilitate the co-op funding and the advertising through an office manager. Make sure you ask the right questions here to ensure you don't have to backtrack after your initial meeting. For example:

- What brand do you sell the most?
- What is the name of your distributor?
- May I have the contact information of your distributor sales representatives?

Remind the office manager that you need this information so you can locate and facilitate the funds for advertising through the distributor's sales representative.

Heating and Air Conditioning Brand Plan Selling Leads

Carrier   Trane   Lennox

Jewelry

Like most categories you are always looking for a category line with the most co-op funding. In a jewelry store, I head immediately to the watches. It's a great place to start the conversation about manufacturer funding with your prospect because most watch brands have formal, paying plans. From there, once you have introduced the concept of co-op funding, you can launch into the conversation about other categories in the store like diamonds, pearls, charm bracelets, and giftware—all have manufacturer funding programs available.

Look for the seasonality for advertising prospects with Valentine's Day, Mother's Day, Father's Day, graduation, and most importantly, the fourth quarter. Nationally, jewelers generate over 23% of their annual sales in December alone.

The single largest growth in this category, in my opinion, has come in the increased demand for charm bracelets, which creates an opportunity. However, I still recommend that you target wristwatches because of the greater availability of formal co-op programs.

Jewelry Brand Plan Selling Leads
Hearts on Fire Diamonds   Rolex Watch
Hummel Figurines

Optical

An often-overlooked category, local opticians and eyewear centers have meaningful co-op accruals in both frames and contact lenses. When engaging your optical prospect, be sure you don't make it more difficult than it needs to be. Although there appears to be dozens of brands represented, most manufacturers have multiple brands. The co-op for those multiple brands is accrued under one manufacturer and can be utilized to advertise any or all of the frame brands. Opportunity!

Most co-op accruals are based on current year sales, making it problematic to tap into funds early in the year, as they haven't earned any yet. This works for that particular industry as most opticians and optical retailers advertise heavily in August when they feature Back to School campaigns. Then, for the remainder of the year through December, they advertise Flex Plan Insurance Spending, which features upgrading frames and prescriptions on insurance dollars that may be expiring.

Optical Brand Plan Selling Leads

Marchon Eyewear   Safilo   Essilor

Flooring and Carpeting

There have been significant shifts recently in flooring and carpeting co-op plans. The hardwood flooring category used to feature plans with most manufacturers participating. We have seen that well of funds dry up. Most of the current funding is for carpeting and area rugs. Of those plans available in carpeting, many of those manufacturers put sales minimums in place to qualify for the co-op funding. Some manufacturers have instituted either a minimum amount of square yards to qualify and others have established minimum sales volume. Even with those changes, we still find installers and retailers everyday with significant available accrued co-op funds.

Target those retailers that have a strong commitment to one or two nationally known and trusted brands. They are the most likely candidates to qualify for funding. You will be able to spot these opportunities often from outside the store with lit signage or banners featuring brands.

Flooring and Carpeting Brand Plan Selling Leads
Karastan Carpet   Shaw   Mohawk

Hunting and Fishing

Hunting, fishing and wildlife viewing contribute more than $3 billion annually to our economy. Many rural markets tend to have more independent firearms dealers. You will want to consult with management before prospecting this category as many media outlets choose not to advertise firearms. Certainly in some parts of the country, hunting and fishing are simply a way of life. If you are going to prospect this category, you will find many manufacturers with meaningful co-op programs.

When you're talking to your firearms dealers, make sure your conversation includes not only firearms, but also ammunition, sport optics, archery, accessories, and fishing brands.

Warning: I once walked into a firearms dealer with my black suit and briefcase in tow. They may think you are visiting from a governmental agency! One of my favorite clients to work with issued a stern warning to me about having your initial meeting with them in that kind of attire so to this very day, whenever I am cold calling any retailer in the hunting and fishing category, I take the time to remove my coat and tie and leave the briefcase in the car before introducing myself!

Hunting and Fishing Brand Plan Selling Leads

Remington Firearms   Hoyt Archery
Nikon Sport Optics

Pools, Hot Tubs, Spas and Accessories

So, where's the money here, coach? Not where you would expect. The most continual, year round sources of co-op funds in this category are found in the upkeep of the pool and spa—the chemicals. As a young seller,

I used to call the period between April and June "Pool Wars". All of the retailers come on board, touting the benefits of the chemical that they sell. All the major brands have great co-op plans and your retailers will have significant accruals. Accessories like automated pool cleaners, toys, and pool covers also have formal co-op plans associated with them.

Hot Tubs and Spas have co-op available in both the upkeep with including the manufacturer's maintenance chemicals and accessories, as well as the hot tub and spa manufacturers themselves. Most plans are based on a fixed amount of funding on a per-unit-purchased basis.

Pools, Hot Tubs, Spas and Accessories
Brand Plan Selling Leads
Totally Hayward   *Arch Chemicals*   *Caldera Spa*

Pellet Stoves and Fireplace Inserts

Alternative energy source products have seen a significant surge in sales as the price of oil has continued to rise. With that rise in price, homeowners aggressively sought more cost-efficient sources for heating their homes. Pellet stoves can be fed with a variety of alternative fuels, and a fireplace insert conversation turns your old fireplace into a significant source of heat.

Several years ago at peak oil price, many retailers were caught off guard with the sudden increase in demand for the pellet stove, and manufacturers fell several months behind on order fulfillment. The demand leveled off, but we now have more of these retailers in markets across the nation than ever.

Co-op funding is generally accrued on the prior year sales in this category; thus, your prospects have meaningful accrued funds in January to commit for marketing for the coming year. Connect with these prospects in mid-summer to assure you have new campaigns running by fall heating season of each year.

More brands are merging, which leaves you with fewer accrual searches to make with your retailer. Each brand, even though sharing the same parent company with others, will accrue its own co-op funding to use marketing that specific product line. Reimbursements may vary from brand to brand, as well as advertising specifications. Be sure to engage the client and while contacting the manufacturer to get current accruals; ask for updated advertising information as well.

Pellet Stoves and Fireplace Inserts
Brand Plan Selling Leads
Vermont Castings   Regency
Hearth and Home Technologies

Insurance

Independent insurance carriers will often have specially arranged co-op funds available through the regional or district manager for the smaller, niche providers. Of course, the brands that you know and trust in this industry offer co-op plans for their agents. Generally, those plans are a fixed amount, based on the agent's prior year sales volume and their costs are reimbursed at 50% of accrual. The amounts fluctuate—the higher the agent's sales volume, the more funds given. These usually cap out at about $4,000 per agent with 50% reimbursement. That would mean your insurance agent/agency prospect would have a co-op marketing budget of $8,000 annually.

Surprisingly, you will be able to secure funding from the district or regional managers from the independent insurance companies quite often. Get the contact information from your prospect and follow through by sending a brief summary proposal to the district manager. Include reach and demographics as well as bottom line price and the amount you are proposing they reimburse the client.

Insurance Brand Plan Selling Leads

Allstate Insurance   State Farm Insurance
Nationwide Insurance

Alternative Energy

Think green, right? As alternative energy manufacturers continue to develop new and innovative products, we continue to see growth in this category. Although we certainly don't have a plethora of participation with formal co-op plans at this time, look for this category to evolve and, in short order, hundreds of manufacturers will be participating with their retailers, dealers, and installers with co-op plans to assist them with their local and regional marketing.

Make sure you engage the prospect and get the manufacturer sales representative's complete contact information so that you can reach out directly on behalf of your prospect regarding marketing funds. Many of them are very open to the discussion, as they need to have additional marketplace awareness of the features and benefits of alternative energy as well as educating consumers on the return on investment.

Home Improvement

I have always described the home improvement category as a "co-op candy store." There are hundreds of generous plans with as much as 100% reimbursements. Many of your hardware store prospects will have an affiliation with a buying group or franchise, so the funds can be found much easier. Those retailers will receive an annual or quarterly statement of funds earned and available.

Always dig deeper with these prospects. You will often find small amounts of fixed manufacturer funds available from those who only sell to distributors. As a result of the manufacturer not having a direct relationship with the end user, they simply offer a fixed amount funds to each retailer in the nation who carries their product. Regardless of volume, the same amounts of funds are given to each retailer, generally capping out at a ten-store limit. These funds are facilitated by a third party co-op administration company and have to be claimed through them. Reimbursements to the retailer are in the form of a check. The only way for a retailer to be aware of these funds is to have a resource like any media's Co-Op Department or perhaps through the distributor's sales representative.

One thing is universally true, the funds only come to those who ask.

Dig deeper yet. What products do they purchase outside of the franchise warehouse agreement? Usually, we expect an additional paint brand, hardscapes, power equipment, and fertilizers, all with additional co-op funding available to your prospect.

If you have a true independent hardware store as a prospect, you will find dozens off formal plans available through their manufacturers.

KEY LEADING QUESTION: What are your top three brands or what are the top three companies you do direct business with? We ask these questions because this is where the funding is! Start small—don't make locating co-op dollars an overwhelming project for them. When you have success finding funds for the first three brands and running local, reimbursable ad campaigns, then you can move on to the next three brands, and so on. Once you achieve success working with

> *KEY LEADING QUESTION: What are your top three brands or what are the top three companies you do direct business with? We ask these questions because this is where the funding is!*

the first three brands, the client will always be more forthcoming and enthusiastic about sharing account information to locate additional funds.

Look for brand opportunities in doors, windows, insulation, roofing, flooring, interior and exterior paint, interior and exterior lighting, siding, plumbing fixtures, hand tools, power tools, lawn and garden equipment, fertilizers, kitchen and bathroom cabinetry, hardware, and more.

Home Improvement Brand Plan Selling Leads
Benjamin Moore Paint
Owens Corning Fiberglass Insulation
National Hardware

Mattress and Bedding

Whenever you are prospecting a furniture retailer, go straight to the bedding department. There you will find famous, trusted brands that will have co-op funds available for your prospect. Bedding departments advertise very aggressively and have high turn. The retailer sells a tremendous amount of the product, resulting in meaningful accruals. Many of the prospects participate in manufacturer full-color flyer programs that they insert in local print sources, but there are still additional funds available for other media.

Mattress and Bedding Brand Plan Selling Leads

Sealy   Serta   Stearns and Foster

Plan

A method for achieving an end:
an often customary method of doing something:
PROCEDURE c : a detailed formulation of a program
of action

L et's explore the kinds of co-op plans that are
made available by manufacturers. They should
be very straightforward and uncomplicated. Don't
intimidate your prospect with the overwhelming
idea of delving in to figure out a co-op plan and plan
details. The easier you make this process on your
prospect, the better the opportunity you will have
to be viewed as a marketing partner and a valuable
resource for helping them place co-op ads against
current earned funds. They have to use these monies
before they expire so remember, you are the Brand
Plan Sales Consultant and you alone can guide them
through the process effortlessly.

Formal Plan

These are the co-op plans you hope to find for your prospect. The manufacturer has clearly stated guidelines for participation and every retailer/dealer who meets those guidelines qualifies for co-op funding. Not all formal plans are the same. Many have varying percentages of accrual, based on the sales volume of the retailer. Others have reimbursements that vary according to the media used for marketing, and yet others have varying forms of reimbursement. It is crucial to have all of the details in hand before moving ahead with your marketing plan.

Special Arranged Plan

When a manufacturer states they have a Special Arranged Plan that means they are open to looking at individual proposals on a case-by-case basis. It is up to you to put together a clear, concise proposal for consideration. Manufacturer's sales representatives are being constantly bombarded with these requests, so brevity is crucial. Keep the proposal should be kept to one page. Simply state the demographics, reach, and price of the media.

Under Special Arranged Plans, consideration is often given for retailers who have opened a new business, perhaps expanded, added a new location, or reached a milestone anniversary. These events can trigger use of manufacturer development funds (also known as MDF) to be used for local and regional marketing. Special Arranged Funds are tapped into most often when a retailer has just opened, it is very easy for you to make the case that the retailer has no accrual available as they have no buying history so the most likely way to move the needle is for the manufacturer to invest with the retailer in a branded advertising campaign. Typically, these funds are referred to as "startup funds." They only come to those who ask, so don't be shy about getting the manufacturer sales representative's contact information and reaching out to them on behalf of your client.

Fixed and Unlimited Plans

Fixed and Unlimited Plans are simply just that. Some manufacturers offer a fixed amount of funding annually regardless of sales volume. The same amount of funding is made available to a retailer selling one piece of inventory as a retailer who is a high volume dealer. In some co-op categories, these fixed funds are made available on a sliding scale with the fixed funding getting higher for meeting certain sales volumes.

Unlimited Plans are from manufacturers who are willing to match any retailer or dealer, dollar for dollar for all approved media, with no limit. There are precious few manufacturers who are willing to extend unlimited terms.

No Co-Op Plan

Manufacturers often state, "No Co-Op Plan available." It may be due to several factors, but doesn't necessarily mean that they never offer cooperative funding. Seasonality of their product may play a part in a co-op plan being temporarily suspended or, more often, you will find that the manufacturer is offering marketing assistance in ways other than actual dollar match funding. Point of purchase materials, website support, and discounts on invoices, branded clothing, and other promotional materials may be offered in lieu of funding.

lan·guage

a : The words, their pronunciation, and the methods of combining them as used and understood by a community

b : The vocabulary and phraseology belonging to an art or a department of knowledge

Accrual

Accrual is the amount of money that is held in a co-op marketing fund pool for a retailer. When you are making the call with your client to a manufacturer's Co-Op Administrator, you will be asking for the accrual or accrued amount of co-op dollars.

Explain to your prospect that, in partnering to locate their accrued funds, you are helping them take back money for advertising that is theirs. The accrual is built into the cost of the product they purchase so you are simply helping them "take back" the money to use for advertising, which will create new traffic and increase sales.

Accrual Percentage

Accrual Percentage is a percentage of paid invoices. Sometimes, instead of being represented by a percentage it is a fixed or flat dollar amount given to all the retailers who stock or sell the product.

Accrual Period

Accrual Period represents the time frame during which the funds accrue. Be sure to specifically ask the Co-Op Administrator to define the Accrual Period. Accrual Periods can vary from Current Year (funds based on paid invoices since January 1st), Prior Year (funds based on paid invoices from the previous years), or other flexible Accrual Periods like 90 day rolling, 12 month rolling, and previous quarter.

> *The accrual is built into the cost of the product they purchase so you are simply helping them "take back" the money to use for advertising, which will create new traffic and increase sales.*

Performance Period

Performance Period represents the deadline for running the advertising. Having a pre-dated invoice does not qualify in meeting the Performance Period guidelines. If the ads are to run by December 31st, you need to have proof of performance showing that the advertising ran prior to that date.

Claim Period

It is very important as a sales consultant to work with first time co-op users to ensure they meet the Claim Period guidelines. Generally, the Claim Period is within 60 to 90 days of when the advertising ran. That includes the time your client has waited for your invoice and proof of performance, so it is very important to remind them to submit the claim immediately. Manufacturers have very little flexibility on processing overdue claims, and the claim for reimbursement can be denied on the basis of not meeting the Claim Period co-op plan guidelines. This is especially true at the end of the year as manufacturer co-op departments are processing claims to close their year.

I have worked with clients in the recent past that missed claim deadlines. Within the calendar year, you still stand a fair chance of getting the manufacturer to honor the claim as, at the end of the day, the retailer is their customer. It is another case altogether once the year has ended, in most cases, the books were closed and there was nothing the Co-Op Administrator could do to assist with reimbursing the claim. I have gotten exceptions for clients that missed the deadline for claiming through year end but they are rare indeed.

> *Bottom line: Make sure your client gets their claim in immediately after they receive proof of performance from your media.*

Bottom line: Make sure your client gets their claim in immediately after they receive proof of performance from your media.

Form of Reimbursement

Every client wants to know how they are being reimbursed and it's very important for you to get the information from the Co-Op Administrator when having the conversation about accrual amounts.

More and more manufactures are working with a Credit Memo. If your client has a $1,000 marketing invoice with a 50% reimbursement rate, assuming they have adequate accrual, the administrator will simply go into the client's account and post a $500 credit. This is essence is the same as cash as it is subtracted from the amount the client owes the manufacturer. If they have no outstanding balance with the manufacturer, the reimbursement would be posted as a credit against a future order.

Other Forms of Reimbursement include a check (which can take up to 12 weeks to process), coupons for the accrued amount good for purchase of product, and actual product equal to the value of the accrual amount. As always, be sure to double-check the Form of Reimbursement as some manufacturers have very "creative" reimbursement solutions.

Advertising Specifications

What needs to be included in the advertising? Depending on your media, the requirements will be different, but you can usually count on several things. The manufacturer often requires brand exclusivity, brand mentions, a feature and benefit statement and also finance and/or safety disclaimers on products like automotive, motorcycles and ATV's. If you are using print media, it will require an appropriate sized logo.

My experience with web banner co-op has been that manufacturers have shown they are very flexible on both content and compliance. With many of the calls I have made on behalf of retailers wanting to use their accrued co-op for web initiatives the manufacturers have approved them, ultimately deciding if it's important to the retailer then they are willing to approve. Bottom line, always ask.

Always e-mail the completed advertisement to the Co-Op Administrator for written pre-approval. In this day and age, it takes precious little time to send the ad over to guarantee the ad complies with the manufacturer's guidelines. When you receive the e-mail with the written pre-approval, forward it to your client so they can enclose it with the proof of performance when they send in their claim for reimbursement.

Co-Op Administrator

The Co-Op Administrator is the person who is responsible for administering the co-op program for the manufacturer. This person is the contact for the accrual information as well. Accrual is a function of the accounting department, not marketing, as accrual amounts are directly tied to paid invoices. Your prospect will have the name and contact information for their manufacturer sales representative. Although manufacture sales representatives are valuable, when they are contacted regarding co-op accruals, the sales representatives generally will call the manufacturer's Co-Op Administrator and report back results to the retailer. It's simply easier to go directly to the Administrator.

When you are making a call for accrual research to the Co-Op Administrator, don't waste their time by not making the call with your client. This information is sensitive and should only be given with the consent of the retailer. The quickest, most efficient way to get current accruals is to make the call to the administrator while on speaker phone together, so both you and your prospect can interact on the call. This method of working with the prospect on finding current accruals will give you instant results and help you to move towards closing a sale without a return visit.

> *The quickest, most efficient way to get current accruals is to make the call to the administrator while on speaker phone together, so both you and your prospect can interact on the call. This method of working with the prospect on finding current accruals will give you instant results.*

You can also make accrual requests from the Co-Op Administrator via e-mail but it will require you to have a signed authorization letter on the retailer's letterhead. The authorization form should include a short paragraph about the prospect, giving you permission to check accrual on their behalf and also include all contact information on the prospect, including account number.

If you or your retailer doesn't know who the Co-Op Administrator is, don't panic. Simply call the manufacturers main number, ask for the Marketing Department and then ask for the person that is responsible for maintaining co-op accrual data.

Claim Requirements

The claim requirements will vary depending on your media. You need to make sure that your client receives all of the necessary documents so that they can send their claim to the manufacturer as soon as possible after the advertising has run. Claim requirements include an additional original invoice, a full page tearsheet for print, a notarized avadavat stating the actual spot dates, times and prices and a copy of the script for radio claims.

Each manufacturer has specific claim requirements. Check with the Co-Op Administrator when you have them on the phone getting the updated accrual data to make the advertiser clearly understands what they need to get reimbursed.

con·flict

a: competitive or opposing action
of incompatibles : antagonistic state or action
(as of divergent ideas, interests, or persons)

It's hard to believe but we encounter obstacles every day when we are introducing the concept of co-op advertising to prospects. Most of those are overcome easily and are simply a defense because they don't understand co-op or have had a bad experience in the past.

> *Most of those are overcome easily and are simply a defense because they don't understand co-op.*

Remember, while it is important to overcome objections to using the retailer's co-op, if they are not engaged and not showing buying signs then the point is moot. All you are going to do is educate them on how to use it with the media they prefer.

◆ **We don't have any co-op**

This is often the first refrain we will hear when we introduce the idea of co-op funding. There are thousands of manufacturers with participating plans, it is virtually impossible for them or us for that matter, to be able to assume that the retailer doesn't have any co-op.

Always ask the retailer for the manufacturer sales representative's contact information. This is the person that sells to your retailer and has a vested interest in your retailer both advertising and selling more of their product(s).

Engage the prospect and promise them after you get a list of stocked brands that you will investigate and report back any results. Even if there isn't a co-op plan in your database you will follow up with the manufacturer sales representative to see if that have market development funds available.

◆ **We have all of our co-op completely under control**

If I only had a dollar for every time I have heard this! The retailer has their co-op under control is code for, we are using the easy and largest plans from out top vendors. Time after time I find that the retailer is only using one or two brands with funding and have no idea that they have several other products with formal co-op plans and additional funding is available. Always dig deeper, this will pay off for you.

Time after time I find that the retailer is only using one or two brands with funding and have no idea that they have several other products with formal co-op plans and additional funding is available.

❖ **We don't like the manufacturer ads they make us use**

Using the manufacturer ads are the easy way out and not necessarily required. It's not unreasonable that the content is going to be exclusive to the manufacturer as they are generally reimbursing the retailer for at least 50% of the total ad cost.

Ask the Co-Op Administrator when you have them on the phone if you can use your own creative as long as you promise to get it pre-approved through them. 9 times out of 10 it's not a problem although there are manufacturers who will only approve content they have created.

Some manufacturers will vary the co-op reimbursement depending on if the ad is dealer/retailer created versus using manufacturer content. It is not unusual to see a co-op plan that offers 100% reimbursement if you use manufacturer content and 50%

reimbursement if you use the retailers creative. The manufacturer is willing to reimburse a higher percentage as they would prefer that the brand message being delivered regionally marries that of the national advertising campaigns they are running.

◈ Our brands don't have co-op available

They may not but you have to check. Get a list of your prospects top brands, investigate and report back the results as soon as possible. Some categories don't traditionally have co-op funding but most do. Other times I have been pleasantly surprised after following up with the manufacturer's sales representative to find out that they do have a co-op initiative that I simply was not aware of. New plans are being developed daily so it's crucial that you follow through with every lead.

◈ We take a discount on invoice instead of having co-op

Some manufacturers offer the retailer a discount on invoice in lieu of a formal co-op plan with reimbursement. We often find discount on invoice deals when a prospect is buying from a distributor. It would be time consuming for a distributor to sort through each retailer's purchases by brand and then give co-op for the appropriate amount of funding on each.

◆ **We use our co-op for displays and apparel**

That's great but does it create traffic and create sales? No. Giving sweatshirts with the manufacturer logo on them to contractors will not grow sales and market share. Having manufacturer displays in the store will not help you bring customers in to your store, they are already there. Appeal to your prospects good business sense in explaining that they only way to grow their business is to use the available co-op funding to advertise.

I have recently worked with a major ski area and found the bulk of their co-op arrangements from manufacturers were in product trade. We talked about why it made more sense to negotiate actual co-op funds for marketing to increase traffic and sales. The very next season they were able to sign agreements for marketing dollars with countless manufacturers and increase the advertising budget three fold with the manufactures reimbursing 50 percent of the cost.

◆ **We use all of our co-op in the newspaper**

Most manufacturers have traditionally designed pre-approved advertising slicks in the appropriate column sizes for daily newsprint, thus making it a very easy form of media to use. All the retailer needs to do is have the media add the dealer tag.

You need to make it just as easy for the prospect to use their co-op with you. Take the time to write a script or get a spec print ad done. Take it one step further and get it pre-approved by the manufacturer and you can almost guarantee you will close the sale.

◆ We would like to use our co-op, but we don't know how much we have

What a great opportunity for you to partner with the prospect. Get the manufacturer co-op contact information and make the call together. Simply let the administrator know that you are with the retailer and you are requesting the current co-op accrual. Also be sure to find out the reimbursement percentage and if you need to send the ad to them for pre-approval.

◆ We used co-op before and didn't get reimbursed

Why didn't they get reimbursed? Was it a problem with the claim procedure, did they not have funds available, did they not get the ad pre-approved? Any of these could be the reason that they were not reimbursed. Your job is to walk them through the process to make sure this doesn't happen to them again. Call the manufacturer and confirm the accrual. Send the ad for written pre-approval. Follow up after and make sure they have received everything they need from you to send in their claim on a timely basis.

Usually when we hear this objection it happened many years ago, sometimes decades before. With the use of the internet the process is streamlined and many manufacturers have web portals with all of this information on it, including accruals, pre-approved materials and claiming.

✦ The paperwork is too confusing

Most of that paperwork has been eliminated with single sheet claim and online claim forms.

✦ We don't want to run ads with only one product in them

You can run a portion of the ad featuring the brand and as long as it is not a competing product the manufacturer will allow you to have another product in the advertisement. The manufacturer will reimburse based on the percentage of the overall ad space you used for their product.

I would suggest that you talk about why it makes sense to advertise brands and have the client run or rotate several different ads featuring individual products.

⬧ **Our manufacturers have never mentioned co-op so we are sure we don't have any**

Not true! There are thousands of manufacturers who offer formal co-op plans and the retailers simply have not been educated. Many manufacturers send information regarding signing up for co-op plans at the beginning of the year and they were overlooked by the retailers. Other manufacturers simply don't get the information out at all and retailers have to be savvy enough to ask. Teach your retailers to starting ASKING every manufacturer representative they see or speak to if there is a co-op plan in place they can take advantage of.

> *The time to negotiate co-op "start up funds" is when the retailer is negotiating with the manufacturer sales representative prior to the initial product order.*

In the end, it's a win for everyone, the retailer will get funding, they will in turn place more advertising and sell more product, which in turn will lead them to ordering more product from the manufacturer and accruing more co-op to advertise with!

Educate your retailer that often co-op only comes to those who ask, especially when they are committing to carrying a new product line. The time to negotiate co-op "start up funds" is when the retailer is negotiating with the manufacturer sales representative prior to the initial product order.

✦ Co-Op isn't what it used to be

Co-Op is exactly what it has always been as co-op funds are expressed as a percentage of current or prior year sales, if the retailer's sales are lower than they used to be, they are going to have a lower accrual.

There are as many co-op plans as there have ever been. When a retailer expresses this concern, share the fact that if they buy more merchandise or buy at the levels they did previously, they will have the co-op accruals that they used to have.

dis·cov·ery

1*a*: the act or process of discovering
b (1)archaic: DISCLOSURE *(2)obsolete:* display
cobsolete: EXPLORATION

2: something discovered

THE THREE QUESTIONS

You only need to ask these three leading questions to tap into any funds your prospect may have available. Engage your client, once you feel they are interested in your product then you can introduce co-op into the conversation. Ask these three questions and they will lead you to the money.

1. What Are Your Top Three Brands?

Why ask this question? This is where the money is. You are going to increase your chances of finding the most meaningful accruals by working with your prospects top three brands. After you have researched those three brands and had success I can guarantee you the retailer will be forthcoming with information on the next three brands.

> *You only need to ask these three leading questions to tap into any funds your prospect may have available.*
>
> 1. *What Are Your Top Three Brands?*
> 2. *Do You Buy Direct?*
> 3. *If Not, Who Is Your Distributor and What Is Your Distributor Representatives Contact Information?*

2. Do You Buy Direct?

Co-op funds follow the chain of the sale and can stop anywhere in that chain. Distributors are not obligated to pass funds through. If your prospect buys direct then you need to find out what the manufacture's contact name and number is and simply call them when you are sitting with your retailer to get the current co-op accrual.

3. If Not, Who Is Your Distributor and What Is Your Distributor Representatives Contact Information?

You need to get the distributor information and follow up to see if they pass through co-op funds. Categories like tires, heating and air conditioning traditionally pass funds through to the retailer/installer. Others like pet and beauty products don't generally have pass through funds. You need to ask, no exceptions, you never know what you will find.

con·ver·sa·tion

1 obsolete: CONDUCT, BEHAVIOR

2a (1): oral exchange of sentiments, observations, opinions, or ideas *(2)*: an instance of such exchange : TALK <a quiet *conversation*>

WHERE CAN FOUND FUNDS BE USED?

All co-op plans are not approved for usage with all forms of media. Daily newsprint continues to be the most universally excepted form of media with internet plan development on the rise. Traditional media like radio, direct mail and television continue to be eligible for the majority of manufacture co-op plans. Over the past several years manufacturers have started developing more pre-approved web banners.

Because many media types are approved for the same manufacturer co-op plan you need to make sure that your prospect is engaged and showing you signs of buying before you share plan details and start making accrual inquiries with the prospects vendors.

Otherwise the client will use the information that you have provided to advertise using co-op with your competitor. Nothing will make your day more than seeing one of your prospects co-op ads pop up in a competing media which is why you always need to be painfully aware that although you are assisting with facilitating the co-op, the funds belong to the retailer and they can spend them in any way they see fit.

Co-Op can be used for, but not limited to, the following media types:

- Daily Newsprint
- Radio
- Direct Mail
- Event Marketing
- Internet
- Weekly Newsprint
- Television
- Billboards
- Point of Purchase Materials

HOW TO HAVE THE CO-OP CONVERSATION

Call on Cell from client's location, on speaker phone and WITH client present

"Good morning Jean" (Co-Op Administrator)

"This is Tim calling with John" (owner/manager of business)

"Can you please give us the current co-op accrual?"

"The account number?" "Sure, John can you give her your account number?"

"Thank you Jean, a couple of things quickly if we can, can you forward any current marketing information to John?"

"Please tell us what the reimbursement percentage is and when the funds expire?"

"Thank you and we will forward the marketing information John and I come up with to you for your preapproval."

Co-Op can be used for, but not limited to, the following media types:

- *Daily Newsprint*
- *Radio*
- *Direct Mail*
- *Event Marketing*
- *Internet*
- *Weekly Newsprint*
- *Television*
- *Billboards*
- *Point of Purchase Materials*

What do you do if you don't make contact with the Co-Op Administrator?

Leave a message for them to return the call with the current co-op accrual to John (her customer)

It's that simple. Don't over complicate the process. Keep it limited to three plans and it should take you no longer than a few minutes with each Co-Op Administrator call. After the call you will have all the information you need and you can in turn, make advertising decisions on the spot as you will have the updated co-op accruals.

> *It's that simple. Don't over complicate the process. Keep it limited to three plans and it should take you no longer than a few minutes with each Co-Op Administrator call.*

You need to get a commitment from the prospect while you are sitting with them. If you walk out of the room you are leaving them the opportunity to use the found accrued funds in another media.

suc·ceed

1 [*no obj*] **a:** to do what you are trying to do : to achieve the correct or desired result • You can *succeed* where others failed. • She hopes to *succeed* [=to do well] at her job.— often + *in*] • Our team *succeeded in* stopping their offensive momentum. • **b:** to happen in the planned or desired way • The plan just might *succeed*. • Their attempt seemed unlikely to *succeed*.

2 a [+ *obj*] : to come after (something) in a series • The new model will *succeed* [=*replace*] the current one next spring.

New Business Using Co-Op

You can create new business by being aware of brands in your territory. Look for signage in the form of banners, posters, neon signs, door decals, pamphlets, point of purchase materials and more. You can also prospect for new co-op business in competing media by looking or listening for advertising that features brands.

Try prospecting by category, focus, one thing at a time. Go on line and get a list of all the retailers in your territory that carry a specific category of product, i.e. heating and air conditioning. Make direct, face to face contact with each dealer and discuss marketing strategies using available co-op funding.

When you have identified co-op in other media, introduce the subject of using co-op to offset the cost of advertising with you. Assume the co-op in your first conversation.

"I am sure you are aware that Serta offers co-op that will offset the cost of advertising with us by at least 50%. We can work together and get an ad pre-approved and I will make sure you get all the proper paperwork for your claim after the ad runs."

Writing Effective Proposals Using Co-Op

Always assume available co-op when you are writing a proposal for a prospect with brands. They will educate you if they have already used the available co-op or if they don't have any funds. Do not mislead your prospect into thinking they have funds that you have not confirmed. Make sure you talk to them about "possible" or "potential" co-op that should be available.

Grow Co-Op Accruals and Advertising Budgets

When you are working with a prospect, one of the primary tips to keep in mind is that the co-op accrual you find has nothing to do with the amount of advertising the client needs. The accrual number simply represents a percentage of the prospects purchases from the manufacturer.

For years I fell into the trap of finding a client $1,000 at 50% and proposing they spend $2,000 to max out the available co-op. What I found by doing this is that the retailer was often not happy with the results of the advertising and didn't want to renew. Why? We are the advertising professionals. It's our job to present a proposal that is going to increase traffic and create sales. How can we do that? Only by offering them an advertising campaign with frequency are we going to create the desired results for the retailer.

> *It's our job to present a proposal that is going to increase traffic and create sales. How can we do that? Only by offering them an advertising campaign with frequency are we going to create the desired results for the retailer.*

- *Buy more advertising*
  - *Increase customer count and sales*
- *Increased sales means they need to order more product*
- *Ordering more product means they will accrue more co-op*
  - *Accruing more co-op means the retailer can buy more advertising*
  - *And the cycle repeats itself with accruals getting larger and larger over the years*

Good news, we have found $1,000 for a client. Share the found accrual with them along with your proposal. You may propose $4,000 in advertising and you need to share with the client that they will be getting $1,000 of that back after the put in their claim for reimbursement.

This puts your client into the Co-Op Increased Accrual Cycle and next time you check accruals they will have a larger accrual to help offset the cost of more advertising!

- Buy more advertising
- Increase customer count and sales
- Increased sales means they need to order more product

- Ordering more product means they will accrue more co-op
- Accruing more co-op means the retailer can buy more advertising
- And the cycle repeats itself with accruals getting larger and larger over the years

Success Stories

Today I went to a current client. After simply mentioning the word co-op my client said "sure, I have some co-op for my cigar brands, I just don't bother to use it as it's not very much." It turns out he had almost $2,000 at 50% and I was able to put together a plan for an additional $5,000 in advertising!

I was able to close a deal today for a small hardware store chain. He owns three stores and although he was aware of the co-op that he gets from his warehouse purchases, he was not aware of co-op that he accrues for the products he buys directly. We were able to find him funds in lawn care products, hand tools, interior and exterior paint and gas grills. He had not advertised with us for years and we are thrilled to have him back!

Thanks to the training I had a conversation with a prospect about Regency Fireplace Inserts. After making a call to Regency with the client I discovered that the process was not scary at all, as a matter of fact the girls at Regency were very nice. The client signed up on the spot and I am sure we will be working together for many years now. We have also started exploring other brands that I am sure will pay off for us.

From one visit I was able to get a current advertiser to run something other than pool openings and closings for the first time by using available Hayward Pool Chemical funds. They had used some in the past but had buying point of purchase materials and branded clothing with the funds. We were able to find a bit over $4,700 and got them to use it all!

I met with the Doctor today and we are moving forward with running advertising featuring three of his brands. This is the first advertising we have done featuring brands and we are using it to supplement the ads he has already been running.

I was able to close a deal today using Raynor Garage Doors by securing funding for the client to use for advertising with us. We of course offered to work with them to make sure they get all the paperwork they need for reimbursement. They usually find themselves chasing all this paperwork down near the claim deadline so they are excited to have found a true marketing partner in us.

I closed a deal today for $7,000 for a new advertiser using Kioti Tractor co-op. They have been approached many times but by talking to them about co-op we signed a contract for the rest of the year. We called the manufacturer together and got the accrual amount as well as having them forward all of the preapproved advertising materials to us.

Have confidence in yourself and your product and the sale is sure to follow. When they find out that you have a proven way to help them offset the cost of doing the right thing and advertising with you, both you and your client will succeed.

We Don't Sell Co-Op!

Lastly, we don't sell co-op. Sell the benefits of advertising with your media. If the prospect is not interested in your product offering them co-op assistance is not going to close the deal, it's simply going to make it easier for them to use it with your competitor. Have confidence in yourself and your product and the sale is sure to follow. When they find out that you have a proven way to help them offset the cost of doing the right thing and advertising with you, both you and your client will succeed.

- *Sell Your Media Type*
  - Why not, it gets results!

- *Sell Your Specific Media*
  - You are the best of the best

- *Sell Yourself*
  - You are a marketing professional and they are looking to you for guidance

- *Then Sell Using Co-Op*
  - Nothing like getting 50–100% of the marketing paid for by the manufacturer

tes·ti·mo·ny

Firsthand authentication of a fact

EVIDENCE

H ow effective is Brand Plan Selling? Here are some testimonials from actual sellers that are working the Plan and making it part of their everyday sales. After spending thousands of hours at the street level visiting prospects with all kinds of media, one thing always comes shining through—there are always new prospects in every town and

> *After spending thousands of hours at the street level visiting prospects with all kinds of media, one thing always comes shining through—there are always new prospects in every town*

county across the United States that have funding available that they are not using. Sales representatives that work the Brand Plan Selling Process, continue to tap into new revenue year after year.

You are next!

"From the first time I was introduced to the concept of co-op advertising I was always interested in how to tap into the additional money. But up to that point, the information we received was very vague. After meeting The Co-Op Coach, that all changed. I listened very closely and now understand the huge amount of money that is available in my territory that I had been leaving on the table every year. The co-op information is invaluable and gives me a distinct advantage over my competition. In today's 'New World', this is a resource that you can really use to help build your annual sales."

—FRED K.

"My grandfather used to tell me, 'A Jack of all trades is a master of nothin'.' He sold Chevys for 30 years. I believe he was short sighted…. Knowing every brand possible when you engage multiple potential or current advertising clients gives you an instantaneous edge. A perfunctory appearance of knowledge of the guts of that business, even if all you know is their BRAND. People identify with brands, especially when they write checks to that name BRAND

every week or month. Now use more BRANDS and get them to write more checks to YOU!"
—Chris C.

"The co-op knowledge provided by Tim Marceau, The Co-Op Coach, has given me a real edge in helping clients maximize their co-op marketing funds. When you can find dollars that clients have accrued to use towards promoting their business, you not only get the buy, you earn their trust for future marketing campaigns. Clients feel that you are making the effort to help their business, not just sell them advertising."
—Mike M.

"I have worked with a pool retailer for several years … they do not install pools. They do pool openings and closings as well as repairs and sell a major spa brands. They utilize co-op for both pool chemicals and spas. In total, they get an average $8,000.00 to $12,000 annually in Co-Op Credits. By utilizing their co-op dollars, they were able to save enough money to hire a part-time service person and they have increased profit considerably by being able to log more service hours for both pool openings and closings, and regularly scheduled weekly service. Having done so, they now sell more chemicals and spas so now they are in turn receiving more annual co-op funds!
—Tim K.

"There's strength in numbers. I brought together a group of individual hardware stores who have co-op from their warehouse distribution chain. Each retailer has an annual allotment of funds. Bring a group of dealers together by offering them a shared co-op plan. Each dealer is responsible for a portion of the advertising schedule and that cost is further reduced by using co-op funds. Dealers share tags, along with the overall cost of the advertising.

Many auto dealers don't use their co-op funds because they are unsure how to use co-op. Offer to assist them with getting pre-approved advertising and you'll most likely have a monthly buy for years to come. After training with the Co-Op Coach, this is what I do: ask to see their dealer funds balance report and make a plan to use up the funds that expire each month. Write up a script using the manufacturer's website information, get it approved by the manufacturer's co-op division, and run the schedule. Match up your invoices and co-op paperwork, get dealer's signature, and send it in for reimbursement to client. Most of the time, these payments are in the form of a credit towards what they are already purchasing from the manufacturer so my dealers love this additional service our media offers them! I use my co-op knowledge to set myself apart from other sellers in my territory."

—Sheila B.

"Co-op brings me lots of additional revenue! It also helps to use co-op when you are pressing for extra sales before the end of the month, working with clients need that need to use their co-op funds before they expire. If you don't have co-op training and a resource, you will not know which co-op plans these are!"

—Nicole D.

"Whether it be 'breaking the ice' or finding more funds from an existing client, the knowledge that The Co-Op Coach brings to the meetings is second to none. With Co-Op, we have taken a potential client and made them fully commit due to the knowledge Tim brought to the table regarding the products they have and the current paying co-op plans that were offered. I have also seen him turn a good client to a great client because of his aforementioned knowledge of plans and manufacturer contacts. Tim is a resource, a motivator, and more a valued business partner in everything I do in my daily selling."

—Keith H.

"Each time I help local business owners uncover additional co-op dollars, I end up finding other business owners with the same product and additional co-op dollars. There's nothing more exciting than finding more money on the table, and that's the beauty of recognizing co-op."

—Paula H.

"Utilizing co-op has been very successful for me with my existing clients, along with a GREAT way of prospecting. Over the years of working with The Co-Op Coach, we have opened many doors to potential clients that were previously closed, but then the conversation about co-op advertising caught the attention of the client. If you follow the guidelines that The Co-Op Coach has established, I don't see any reason why it won't work for you, and your clients will benefit from doing business with you! Don't prequalify your clients on what you think they may have for co-op based on what industry they represent, size, or location. Follow the steps, do the research, make the calls, ask the questions, and you, too, will help address your clients' needs through advertising with your media and have the manufacturers pay for some or all of it!"

—Glen N.

Contact

If you would like The Co-Op Coach come visit your media and share the, Co-Op ~ A Bright Idea presentation, please go to www.theco-opcoach.com for contact details.

Invest one day and your sales staff will be having co-op fund conversations with current and past advertisers as well as prospecting in a new way and profitable way. Once they have tuned into the co-opportunities in their territory the new revenue possibilities are endless!